FLORA IN FOCUS
TROPICAL GARDENS

TIGER BOOKS INTERNATIONAL
LONDON

This edition published in 1996 by
Tiger Books International PLC, Twickenham

Photographs:
PPWW Plant Pictures World Wide, Daan Smit
Text:
Nicky den Hartogh
Translation:
Tony Langham
Concept, design and editing:
Boris van Dobbenburgh
Typesetting:
Mark Dolk/Peter Verwey Grafische Produkties
Color separation:
Unifoto PTY LTD, Cape Town
Production:
Agora United Graphic Services bv, 's-Graveland
Printing and binding:
Egedsa, Sabadell, Spain

ISBN 1-85501-828-4

INTRODUCTION

Increasingly people can afford to travel to distant countries. Since it has become possible to travel from Europe to hot, tropical regions by air, the journey takes so little time that holidays are sufficient for acquiring a first, unforgettable impression of a foreign country, its inhabitants and culture, its flora and fauna.

It is a first impression, no more than that. Even if the traveler limits himself to a specific area, such as, for example, the two Indonesian islands of Java and Bali, the journey can be stimulating enough to provide enjoyment for years. Temple complexes have been built in the most magnificent spots, with courtyards and terraces which blend and become one with the surrounding landscape. They seem to give an extra dimension to the beauty of nature. The most beautiful flowering shrubs and trees are planted next to the countless house altars. In the famous botanical gardens (Kebun Raya) at Bogor on Java alone, there are ten thousand different varieties of trees. There are gardens planted in the colonial style like parks, as well as contemporary hotel gardens and private gardens.

To think that Java and Bali are only two of the countless sights there are to see. The tropics actually cover large areas of Asia, South America and Africa. Even for the most enthusiastic visitor of gardens it would be impossible to visit all the places which display the magnificent range of the tropical plant world.

The tropics form a broad band around the equator between the Tropic of Cancer and the Tropic of Capricorn, though they do not form an enclosed whole. In the coldest month of the year the temperature does not fall below 65°F. According to the generally accepted classification of Vladimir Koppen, they can be divided into two main zones: areas with a tropical rainforest climate, and areas with a savannah climate. Together these account for approximately 20% of the earth's total land surface area. Central Africa, parts of Brazil and Venezuela, and the interior of South and Southeast Asia are influenced by the savannah climate. For part of the year the climate is humid, but the winters are fairly dry. There are wide plains of park-like landscapes, with grasses and occasional groups of trees. The Congo basin in Africa, the Amazon basin in South America, a narrow strip of Central America, parts of the Far East, Indonesia and other tropical islands and coastal areas enjoy the tropical rainforest climate. This is characterized by a fairly constant humidity and heat. Even in the driest month, there is at least a little rain.

There are also areas where vegetation flourishes despite the dry season, because the earth always remains sufficiently moist during the periods following heavy rainfall. This is known as a monsoon climate.

The hot, "humid" tropics have the greatest variety of flora in the world. Most tropical garden plants come from these areas.

It is no more possible to characterize tropical gardens in general terms than it is possible to do so for gardens in temperate climates. The influence of particular cultures, eras and religions has resulted in countless styles of garden architecture.

Although there are differences in plant growth because of the composition of the soil and different climatological influences, the same plants can be cultivated in vast areas. It is certainly not the case that most plants in gardens and trees by the roadside are indigenous to the country where they are found. In that respect, the same applies in the tropics as in Europe: many ornamental plants come from far away, and have become so common in the countries where there were introduced over the years, that they have become part of the familiar landscape. Even the frangipane (Plumeria rubra), which has been planted next to temples in Asia since time immemorial, does not originate from there at all. The tree came from Central America.

The flamboyant (Delonix regia), which has a crown covered with magnificent red flowers when it is blossoming, belongs to the indigenous flora of Madagascar. However, the flamboyant is such a common tree on the streets and in the parks of tropical countries, that it is impossible to imagine the landscape without them.

Holidaymakers from Europe will find something they recognize in a number of tropical plants: a familiar fruit, cut flowers, pot plants or greenhouse plants. Nevertheless, many people are quite astonished when they see these plants growing in hot countries for the first time. The enormous, forceful growth which characterizes the plant world in the humid tropical climate is particularly striking. We think of Ficus benjamina as being very tall when the crown reaches the ceiling of the living room, but in tropical Asia it can grow into a large tree with an awesome system of aerial roots which serve as a tree trunk. In Indonesia, the weeping fig, as this ficus variety is known, is believed to be inhabited by gods. It is found in temple gardens, next to houses, and in squares, amongst other places, and is important as a tree which provides shade.

Tall palm trees, tree ferns and cycas palms grow in such a different way from "ordinary trees" that they create a completely different atmosphere than in the cool regions of temperate zones. The Pandanus or screw pine, with its strange prop roots above the ground and characteristic foliage, also determines the special character of tropical gardens. This tree (for Pandanus is actually not a palm) is often planted in eye-catching spots in gardens and parks, and makes an excellent wind-break in coastal regions.

It is striking to see how often flowers are red in the tropics. In the natural world the colors and fragrance of flowers normally serves to attract particular pollinators which transfer the pollen from one flower to the pistil of another.

Various trees and plants with red flowers, including Erythrina varieties and Heliconias, are pollinated by birds in their country of origin.

Although there are many shrubs, trees and herbs which flower abundantly, the beauty of tropical gardens is by no means always determined primarily by flowers. When the garden is planted, an important factor is also the great diversity of trees and leafy plants which can be used to achieve superb effects of color and shape.

Heliconias with their banana-shaped leaves taller than a man, ornamental Cordylines, the large leaves of ginger plants, Dracanenas, Philodendrons and other members of the arum lily family, together form a wealth of jungle-like vegetation, or are displayed to magnificent effect as solitary plants amongst the plants growing lower down. Red and white variegated varieties produce colorful effects. Bromelias with their colored tubular leaves, the partly purplish-red Rhoeo spathacea, Iresine herbstii, and various Coleus varieties, are planted on a massive scale to produce patterns of color.

The ideas of the Brazilian, Roberto Burle Marx, in the field of composition, contrasting shapes, rhythm and color, have particularly served as a source of inspiration for contemporary garden and landscape architects throughout the tropical world. Amongst other things, Burle Marx designed the big city parks in Rio de Janiero, and his gardens are designed in such a way that it is as though the specific characteristics of a plant are drawn out and emphasized more strongly than in their natural environment. In addition, he has in his own country stimulated a revival of interest in the infinite wealth and variety of the indigenous flora. Because of his influence, the art of planning gardens has also developed significantly in tropical regions far from Brazil, and the individual character of the tropical plants has increasingly become the central feature in gardens and public parks.

A RISTOLOCHIA BRAZILIENSIS

Aristolochia species are specialized in catching insects, not because they are carnivorous, but because they need flies and beetles to pollinate them. The large, usually dark colored flowers, have a special shape for this purpose. The sepals form a sort of sac with a narrow entrance and a protruding lip, or broad ledge, which serves as a landing place for insects. When flies go in through the entrance, they go into a sort of curved "lock," which makes it difficult for them to find the way back out because of the hairs growing inwards. In the end the fly is funnelled to the part of the flower containing the pistil and stamens. The pollen collected by the insect from when it landed on another flower now comes into contact with the receptive stigma at the end of the pistil. Shortly afterwards, the pipe flowers on the stamens open up and more pollen lands on the insect. As soon as this has happened, the hairs in the narrow passage of the lock soften, and the insect can get back out to look for another flower. Because of the special shape of certain species, Aristolochia is also known as the pipe flower. In its place of origin, the dried roots of Aristolochia braziliensis, a climbing plant from Brazil, were used in the past as an antidote for snake bites.

DICKSONIA ANTARCTICA

Because they differ enormously from "ordinary trees" in the way they grow, palms, tree ferns and fern palms make a very individual impression on the landscape. Although these tree-like plants are not related from a botanical point of view, they have a lot in common as regards their appearance. They do not form a crown of branches, but are crowned by spreading palm-like fronds at the top of a straight trunk which does not have any branches. In Dicksonia antarctica, the tree fern from Australia and Tasmania, the crown of leaves is composed of double, much-divided, delicately arching leaves, which grow to a length of approximately eight feet. The plant thrives in the shade of high trees and comes into its own both as a solitary plant and in large groups.

VANDA HYBRID

FICUS BENJAMINA

In a garden in Bogor, the slender aerial roots of Ficus benjamina hang down to the ground in veils. Eventually they form roots to serve as supports for the branches of the tree. The "Weeping fig," as this ficus is known in Indonesia, is planted in gardens and parks and on squares, because the enormous system of aerial roots provides protective shade for people. The plant is also used as a natural way of dividing up land. The Weeping fig often spontaneously grows from seed deposited in the fork of a tree by a bird or a monkey, and will then survive for a time on the nutrients in the moisture and humus-rich waste matter which has collected within its reach. As long as the plant is only of a limited size, it does not harm its host in any way. However, later on the widely spreading branches form aerial roots which reach down to the ground. After several decades, the aerial roots start to surround the tree on which the Weeping fig germinated, to such an extent that the host plant is gradually "choked." By the time that the host has rotted away, the supporting roots have become strong enough to independently support the weight of the choking fig.

FICUS BENJAMINA (background)

RAVENALA MADAGASCARIENSIS

Although the idea of a tropical garden evokes a picture of exuberant flowers in many people's minds, the beauty of gardens in hot, humid regions, is often largely determined by the contrasting shapes of green plants. The slender trunks of the Traveler's tree, Ravenala madagascariensis, rise up from the low vegetation of Hymenocallis leaves along a footpath.

They are crowned by a curious fan of long-stemmed leaves. In itself, the leaf is unmistakably similar to that of the banana, a member of the same family, but because of the curiously flat arrangement, the leaves form such a distinct pattern that Traveler's trees can be recognized at a glance. The plant originates from Madagascar, and is cultivated in many tropical regions for its decorative fan-like crown.

◀

CYRTOSTACHYS LAKKA

The exuberant growth of the lipstick or sealing wax palms (Cyrtostachys lakka) is surrounded by flowering Vandas in the flowerbeds of the botanical gardens in Singapore. The leaf bases of the lipstick palm, a palm tree with several trunks which is indigenous to the island of Sumatra, have joined together to form a striking bright-red stem.

PASSIFLORA RACEMOSA

The beautifully shaped flowers of Passiflora racemosa between the small, round leaves of Pilea nummularia. The passion flower can climb up shrubs, trees or fences with the help of tendrils, but grows along the ground if there is no support for it. The old stems are not cut away, because this is where the flowers develop.

CALLIANDRA HAEMATOCEPHALA

The luminous red heads of Calliandra haematocephala from Bolivia are composed of numerous long stamens which protrude a long way beyond the tiny corolla. In hot regions, calliandras have become widespread as ornamental shrubs or trees because of the wealth of blossoms. In English-speaking countries they are known as powder puff. The official name is also significant: Calliandra comes from the Greek, and means "with beautiful stamens."

CALLIANDRA BREVIPES

The silky stamens of Calliandra brevipes, indigenous to Brazil, have two colors and end in small but clearly perceptible pollen balls. The fact that calliandra is closely related to the well-known mimosa plant is apparent not only from the spherical stamen flowers, but also from the delicate, double pinnate leaves which are composed of a large number of very small leaflets.

CAPPARIS CORIACEA

The inflorescence of Capparis coriacea, a caper variety from Africa, has just the same round buds as the true caper shrub (Capparis spinosa), of which the flower buds (capers) are used in cooking. As in the case of Calliandra, the flower owes its beauty to the stamens which protrude far beyond the crown.

PANDANUS FURCATUS

Screw pines (Pandanus species) are amongst the most characteristic plants of tropical zones in the ancient world. When they are planted in a particular place in gardens or parks they create a jungle-like effect. At first sight the trees are reminiscent of palms but the fact that the trunks divide into branches immediately indicates that they do not belong to the palm family. Apart from the striking foliage consisting of long bayonet-shaped leaves, it is above all the supportive roots above the ground which lend the screw pine its unusual appearance. The supportive roots are connected to the underground system of roots and serve to support the trunk. They develop both where the palm trees grow naturally, and when it is cultivated. Even when the plants are cultivated in a greenhouse, they form well-developed aerial roots.

DENDROBIUM BULLENIANUM

In the tropical rainforest trees are host to countless epiphytes. Epiphytes do grow in the tree but, unlike parasites, do not extract any nutrients. In places where little light can penetrate, at the lower levels of the jungle, ferns, mosses and other shade-loving varieties develop on moist trunks and branches. Higher up, within reach of the light, are the orchids. They provide fascinating patches of color between the endless greenery. Dendrobium owes its name to its predominantly epiphytic lifestyle. The term consists of dendron (tree) and bios (life) and therefore means: living on trees. There is such a wealth of shapes in the estimated nine hundred varieties of Dendrobium, that it is virtually impossible to give a general description of these orchids.

DENDROBIUM DENSIFLORUM

Dendrobia have thickened stems which sometimes have so many buds that they almost resemble bamboo. In certain varieties the clumps of flowers are so heavy that the stem bends under the weight as can be seen in Dendrobium densiflorum. This orchid from India, the Himalayas and Indo-China is one of the most beautiful of all the Dendrobium species. Its golden yellow flowers have a diameter of two inches and together form a hanging cluster more than eight inches long.

DENDROBIUM SECUNDUM

Before there is any new growth, some Dendrobia just look like a collection of dry stems, but this soon changes when the first clusters of flowers appear. In the illustration of Dendrobium secundum the flowers are still closed. Because they are arranged so closely together they have a striking appearance despite their relatively small size. The open flowers are more or less bell-shaped. They have an attractive orange-yellow disk which contrasts with the burgundy or bright pink color of the petals. The plant is found in a large area which stretches from the Malaysian Archipelago to the Philippines.

PAPHIOPEDILUM MICRANTHUM

Lady's Slipper (Paphiopedilum species) can easily be distinguished from other tropical orchids by the characteristic shape of the flowers. Where they are found naturally, the plants grow at the bottom level of the rain forest and in the humid, mossy mountain forests in South East Asia. The most unusual part of the flower is the adapted lip, but the top petal - the "flag" - is certainly also a striking feature of Lady's Slipper. The lip has the shape of a shoe, or rather of a slipper. It serves to catch insects. When these fly into the slipper, they deposit the pollen of a flower which they have visited earlier on the stigma. When the insect finds that it is no simple matter to leave this trap through the broad entrance it chooses to leave by the narrow emergency exit at the base of the slipper, where it passes the stamens so that it leaves the flower with some of the sticky pollen on its body.

◀ PAPHIOPEDILUM CALLOSUM

CALAMUS FASCICULATA

The thorny crowns of Calamus fasciculata, a rotan palm. Rotan palms do not have a vertical trunk like most other palms, but form stems with leaves which are six to ten feet long and which climb up other trees to find the light in the tropical rain forests. In order to do this the stems, leaves and often even the inflorescences of Calamus species are covered in countless thorns with which the plants hook onto shrubs and branches. The stems of Calamus manam, the longest variety, can reach a length of five hundred feet. (Rotan palms were essential to the forest people of South East Asia for building their homes and for their wickerwork.) Calamus is one of the most important suppliers of cane, and several different varieties are cultivated on a large scale for this purpose.

PHAIUS TANKERVILLEAE (S.P. BICOLOR, P. BLUMEI)

Like the Lady's Slipper, Phaius tankervilleae (synonym: Phaius bicolor) is an orchid which roots in the ground (terristrial orchid). It is found growing naturally in humid and wet grasslands in tropical Asia. The delicate spreading petals of this sturdy plant are darker in color on the outside than on the inside. The protruding lip, the most characteristic feature of an orchid, is a light or dark pink color.

DILLENIA SUFFRUTICOSA

Dillenia suffruticosa originates in the Malaysian Archipelago. The large leaves of this tall shrub are sometimes used for wrapping up food. Bright yellow flowers up to four inches wide develop on the branches. When the red fruit has burst open it is star-shaped. The seeds in the fruit are encased in a purple husk. They are pecked up by birds as soon as the fruit opens.

COUROUPITA GUIANENSIS

The "Cannonball tree" (Couroupita guianensis) is at its most beautiful when it blossoms, because the numerous long flowering stems develop on the bark of the trunk and on the lower branches, and are not overshadowed by the foliage higher up the tree. They are decked with large sturdy flowers with a diameter of four inches which exude a strong, sweet fragrance, especially at night. In their countries of origin the flowers are pollinated by bats. Later on the curiously shaped fruits, as round and hard as a cannonball, hang under the crown of the tree, closely packed together and heavy enough to make the branches sag under their weight.

GUSTAVIA SUPERBA
G Gustavia superba from the South American countries of Columbia, Panama and Ecuador, is cultivated as an ornamental tree because of its beautiful flowers. The heart of the flower is formed by closely packed stamens curving inwards inside the crown of spreading petals. On the outside the petals are colored pink while the inside is white. The large leaves of this plant can grow to a length of three feet. After flowering the branches bear large berry-like, edible fruit.

LICUALA GRANDIS

Licuala grandis, a lovely small palm tree, grows in the garden of a hotel. At the foot of the palm tree, rosette-shaped Rhoea spathacea have been planted with leaves which are green on one side and a bright purplish-red color underneath. The patch is surrounded by a thin border of grassy Ophlopogon leaves. The palm tree in the middle will never grow to a great height, and has a broad crown of large leaves in relation to its size. The V-shaped pleated leaf segments are particularly striking. They grow from the base to the outer edge of the almost round, undivided leaf segments, rather like rays of light. The palm tree is sometimes called a "ray palm" in order to emphasize this characteristic.

PHILIBERTIA GRACILIS

The bowl-shaped flowers of Philibertia gracilis are arranged in compact clusters. The plant originates from Argentina and forms long thin stems which have heart-shaped leaves and wrap themselves around the branches of neighboring shrubs and trees. Philibertia is cultivated as vegetation on walls, bowers and trellises.

PHAIUS TANKERVILLEAE

Phaius tankervilleae looks magnificent against a background of Philodendron scandens and other creepers. It is an orchid which combines an enormous size with elegance and grace. The impressive leaves can grow to a length of no less than three feet while the flowering stems can grow to a height of more than four feet. Every inflorescence consists of a large number of charming flowers with a diameter of three to four inches. Phaius is very suitable for cut flowers.

PLUMERIA RUBRA F. ACUTIFOLIA

The white flowering frangipane (Plumeria rubra f. acutifolia) is one of the most beautiful tropical ornamental flowering trees. It was originally found only in Central America but once the explorers had crossed the seas of the world and joined distant continents, the tree soon found its way to other tropical countries. In Asia it has been planted in temple gardens for so long that it is now known as the pagoda tree or temple tree and seems to form part of the culture. It is also often found in cemeteries, along broad avenues and on squares. The unusually shaped specimen in the photograph is in Bandung on the Indonesian island of Java.

BOCCONIA FRUTESCENS

The inflorescence of Bocconia frutescens is very reminiscent of the well-known plume poppy (Macleaya caudata), the tall garden plant which is cultivated in Europe. This similarity is not a coincidence; they are closely related. Bocconia frutescens is a shrub or small tree from tropical Africa, while the plume poppy is a herb-like plant and comes from the cooler regions of Asia. Bocconia is cultivated as an ornamental plant, not only for its large, hazy flowering plumes, but also because of its large decorative leaves.

DELONIX REGIA

Even for an experienced traveler, a flowering flamboyant (Delonix regia) is still a worthwhile sight. The tree originates from the island of Madagascar, but has become a very common ornamental tree, providing shade in hot countries throughout the world. It is so widespread in many countries that it has become indigenous. The branches spread out, so that the crown forms a broad canopy, providing welcome shade at the hottest time of the day. In dry periods the flamboyant sheds its delicate pinnate leaves to restrict evaporation to a minimum. Before the leaves start to develop again, the branches are decked with countless scarlet flowers six inches wide. These are followed by pods which can grow to a length of two feet.

PHOENICOPHORIUM BORSIGIANUM

Phoenicophorium borsigianum is a feathered plant which was originally indigenous only in the Seychelles, a group of islands in the Indian Ocean. This palm can only be successfully cultivated in a slightly sheltered position in a humid tropical climate.

Phoenicophorium eventually grows to a height of thirty to fifty feet, and has luxuriant foliage. The finely branched infloresences, up to eighteen inches long, develop at the base of the lower leaves and when they have finished flowering, the red fruit develop there.

STRELITZIA NICOLAI

Strelitzia is also known as the bird-of-paradise flower, a name which clearly refers to the curious shape and extraordinary colors of the inflorescence.
In South Africa, its country of origin, there are five different varieties. Three of these develop palm-like trunks in the course of their lives; Strelitzia is the tallest of these, with a height of twenty-five to thirty feet. The plant has large banana-like leaves and bluish-white or purplish-white flowers which protrude beyond the reddish-brown or blue-black boat-shaped bracts like the crest of a bird.

DILLENIA INDICA

Dillenia indica is an Asian tree with an attractive orange-brown trunk.
From the foot of this trunk, twisting roots spread out in every direction. The flowers have a diameter of six to eight inches. When the white petals have fallen, the remaining sepals develop to completely enclose the fruit. (The fruit is eaten raw, or used to make jelly or refreshing drinks.)

PANDANUS SPECIES

PANDANUS UTILIS

The fruit-bearing crown of Pandanus utilis, a screw pine from Madagascar. A number of Pandanus species are not only valued as ornamental trees for parks and gardens, but are also important for their practical use. The fruit of the variety illustrated here is edible, and therefore the plant is "useful," as is indicated by its species name "utilis." In addition, the leaves provide good quality fiber, which is used for making mats.

LICUALA FLABELLATA

Licuala flabellata is an excellent plant for creating contrasts because of the unusual shape of its leaves. As regards its shape, this dwarf palm contrasts beautifully with the large, closed leaf segments of, for example, Heliconias, or with the delicate foliage of smaller leafy plants.

ROYSTONEA REGIA

Absolutely vertical royal palms line the entrance to the botanical gardens in Singapore. The tall royal palm (Roystonea regia) is generally viewed as one of the most charming palm trees and is planted on a large scale in gardens, parks and avenues. In Cuba, their country of origin, they grow naturally in woods and open areas, where they dominate the landscape. In its country of origin the royal palm is a protected species. It has a clump of long pinnate leaves ten feet long at the top of the trunk which is more than sixty feet tall. The leaf bases form a long, smooth stem under the leaves.

ARISTOLOCHIA TRICAUDATA

A number of Aristolochia species, tropical plants with large flowers, are cultivated as climbing plants or ornamental shrubs. The flowers are formed by characteristically shaped sepals and often exude a clearly perceptible smell of carion. The flowers of Aristolochia grandiflora in the Antilles are exceptionally large. They have a diameter of one foot with a tail two feet long. In many varieties the flowers are characterized by a sac-shaped growth, though this does not apply to the Aristolochia tricaudata in the illustration. The plant from Mexico has a curious appearance because the three sepals end in a long tail. The scientific name of the species, tricaudata, means with three tails.

PANDANUS TECTORIUS

With its thin trunk supported on stilt-like roots and its curious foliage, Pandanus tectorius (synonym: Pandanus odoratissimus) is the most striking plant in this water garden. Pandanus tectorius is one of the main varieties of screw pine. Its natural habitat covers a large part of southern Asia, Polynesia and tropical Australia. The flowers and ripe fruit produce a wonderfully scented oil which is used in all sorts of cosmetics.

E RYTHRINA ABYSSINICA

DELONIX REGIA

MANDAI ORCHID GARDENS, SINGAPORE

The Mandai Orchid Gardens are aimed above all at promoting the cultivation and export of orchids in Singapore, but a significant part of the gardens was designed for displaying the possible uses of all sorts of tropical plants and their cultivated varieties.

The vegetation is awe-inspiring under the influence of the hot, humid climate which prevails on the island (Singapore is only eighty miles from the equator). Because of the contrast with the beautifully mown lawns the luxuriance of the vegetation is emphasized even more strongly.

HIBISCUS ROSA-SINENSIS HYBRID

It is almost inconceivable to visit the tropics without coming across the Chinese rose (Hibiscus rosa-sinensis). These elegant flowering shrubs are extremely popular and are cultivated on a large scale. The specimens can develop into small trees. The Chinese rose has been cultivated for such a long time that it is not possible to determine where exactly it originated; it is presumed that it originated in tropical Asia. When the Portuguese first saw the flowers in the sixteenth century they called it "fulo de sapata," or the shoe flower, because they discovered that they could use the juice to blacken their shoes. The stamens of hibiscus flowers are fused in a long tube which protrudes from the heart and contributes to the flower's beauty. The tube ends in a red divided style and yellow anthers underneath.

HIBISCUS SCHIZOPETALUS

Hibiscus schizopetalus originates in East Africa and grows to a height of approximately ten feet. The slender hanging branches with long pointed leaves have curiously shaped flowers with petals which are serrated like a fringe (schizopetalus means "with divided petals").

PYRROSIA LANCEOLATA
A tree with Pyrrosia lanceolata, an epiphytic fern.
◀

PYROSTEGIA VENUSTA
The climbing plant Pyrostegia venusta (synonym: Bignonia venusta) from Brazil and Paraguay grows on walls, roofs, verandas and trees in large parts of tropical America. The popular names of this plant, flame-vine, flaming trumpet and golden-shower, all refer to the magnificent blossom. (There is a pinkish-lilac Ipomoea flower amongst the orange trumpet flowers in the photograph).

N EPHROLEPIS CORDIFOLIA
This beautifully designed woodland garden shows how
intriguing a modest arrangement of green plants on the shore can be.
The vegetation consists, amongst other things, of palm trees of which
there is a great diversity in shape, height and leaves. On the right in
the foreground the delicate fresh green foliage of Nephrolepis
cordifolia is reflected in the water. This is a charming fern of which
there are several cultivated varieties.

CHRYSALIDOCARPUS LUTESCENS

Chrysalidocarpus lutescens - an attractive feathered palm from Madagascar with several trunks - has become widespread in many tropical regions in the course of time. The photograph shows this palm tree in a private garden in a Javanese village. This palm is sometimes known as the "golden-feather" or "yellow palm" because the arching leaves at the top of the slender, smooth ringed trunks acquire a slightly golden-yellow shade in full sunlight. In temperate regions the Areca palm, as it used to be known, was a popular house plant.

MEDINILLA MAGNIFICA

Medinilla magnifica has a mainly epiphytic lifestyle in its country of origin - the rainforests in the Philippines - and usually grows in trees. This shrub can develop to a height of almost eight feet. The thick squarish twigs are covered with large attractive leaves which grow in pairs. The hanging trusses of flowers are composed of hundreds of small coral red or pink florets. They are even further enhanced by colorful bracts. In gardens this spectacular flowering ornamental shrub is sometimes planted to form a hedge or in the foreground.

BULBOPHYLLUM SIKKIMENSE

With eight hundred to one thousand varieties indigenous to Africa, tropical America, Australia and south east Asia, Bulbophyllum is one of the largest orchid families in the world. There are great differences between varieties as regards growth and the flowers. In Bulbophyllum sikkimense the flowers are always packed so tightly together and arranged in a circle, that they look like a single flower.

MANDAI ORCHID GARDENS, SINGAPORE
A grassy path with border plants consisting of
variegated white Talinum (in the foreground on the left), red
flowering Ixora, red leaved Acalypha and Heliconia leaves
(in the background on the right).

HIBISCUS ROSA-SINENSIS HYBRID

This unusual Hibiscus hybrid was produced by crossing two species: Hibiscus rosa-sinensis and Hibiscus schizopetalus.

IRESINE HERBSTII

Because of its colorful red leaves, Iresine herbstii is eminently suitable for producing some areas of color in flower beds and amongst the plants.
The soft fleshy stems are regularly cut to ensure that there is good ground cover with spreading plants.

ERYTHRINA PRINCEPS

There are approximately one hundred Erythrina species which grow in the tropics and subtropical regions and these include a large number of trees which blossom profusely with magnificent red flowers. In areas where there are often periods of very little rainfall, the trees usually shed their leaves in order to survive the dry season, and the flowers appear on the bare branches before the new leaves develop. Erythrinas blossom most beautifully in regions where there are significant changes in the climate every season. Apart from being cultivated as ornamental trees, they also provide valuable shade on coffee and cocoa plantations. When the tree has flowered, the seeds ripen in ribbed pods. The seeds of some varieties serve as the raw materials of medicines and are sometimes used as stimulants. Erythrina princeps (synonym: Erythrina) is the variety shown in the illustration.

PTYCHOSPERMA MACARTHURII

Ptychosperma macarthurii, a feathered palm with several trunks which grow to a height of ten feet, is indigenous to New Guinea. Because it is relatively small this palm is suitable for cultivation in small gardens. It is best to plant it in a place on its own so that the beautiful fruit is not obscured by the plants around it.

MANDAI ORCHID GARDENS, SINGAPORE
A combination of plants with ornamental leaves is used as the border plants for a lawn in the Mandai Gardens. Different varieties of variegated Dracaenas dominate the arrangement.

HIBISCUS ROSA-SINENSIS "COOPERI"

The many cultivated varieties of the Chinese rose include varieties with different colored flowers and different shaped flowers as well as varieties with unusually colored leaves. Hibiscus rosa-sinensis "Cooperi" has small colorful red leaves and the red flowers do not show up against these.

SCHOTIA BRACHYPETALA

Schotia brachypetala, known as the "tree fuchsia," is a large shrub or small tree with a broad crown in which numerous flowers form elegant plumes.

EUPHORBIA PULCHERRIMA

For people who live in the temperate regions of the Northern Hemisphere, it can be a great surprise to come across the seven-to-ten-foot tall "poinsettia" while on holiday in the tropics. The twigs of Euphorbia pulcherrima (synonym, Poinsettia pulcherrima) end in large, bright-red bracts which attract all the attention. It is the parent plant of a large number of cultivated varieties, including the dwarf variety, which flowers in pot plants at Christmas time. The shrub originates from tropical Mexico and Central America, where it was already cultivated before the arrival of the Europeans. The photograph of this specimen in a Malaysian garden reveals the purple blooms of a Bougainvillaea in the background. The beauty of this shrub, like that of the poinsettia, is determined by the color of the bracts.

PLUMERIA RUBRA "CARMINE FLUSH"

The pink flowering Plumeria varieties of Plumeria rubra are as popular in the tropics as the flowering pagoda tree (Plumeria rubra fa. acutifolia). They both have beautifully scented flowers. In East Asia the frangipane or pagoda tree is a symbol of immortality, because leaves and flowers continue to appear on the branches after the tree has been cut down.

IXORA CHINENSIS

Ixora is found in tropical regions throughout the world. There are no fewer than four hundred varieties, of which a number are cultivated as garden plants and cut flowers. Some can be pruned so precisely that, like Buxus, they can be trained into particular shapes. As its name suggests, Ixora chinensis is indigenous to China. This small evergreen shrub does not grow taller than two and a half feet. It is suitable for borders and for planting in beds.

◀ Dicksonia Antarctica

Bauhinia Blakeana

The pinky-lilac flowers of Bauhinia blakeana give off a wonderful fragrance. Although they have five rather than six petals, they are clearly reminiscent of orchids; Bauhinia is popularly known as the Orchid tree. All the cultivated specimens stem from a single tree in Canton (China). They are reproduced by vegetative reproduction, because the flowers are sterile and do not form any seed.

PLATYCERIUM BIFURCATUM

PLATYCERIUM CORONARIUM

Stag's-horn ferns are very common ornamental plants in the tropics.
Both Platycerium bifurcatum from Australia, illustrated here, and Platycerium
coronarium from Asia are extremely attractive plants because of the profuse
antler-shaped bifurcated leaves. All stag's-horn ferns have an epiphytic
lifestyle. Apart from the bifurcated, spreading or hanging leaves on which the
spore patches develop, the plants have plate-like fronds with which they
attach themselves to trees. Stag's-horn ferns are found in Africa, Asia,
Australia and South America; most varieties grow in tropical rainforests.
Platycerium bifurcatum is one of the few stag's-horn ferns which thrive in a
relatively cool climate. When they are cultivated, the plants are tied onto tree
ferns or onto pieces of bark covered with sphagnum moss or other moist
material. Stag's-horn ferns are also cultivated in hanging baskets or in pots.

HIBISCUS ROSA-SINENSIS

For people in many countries, the charming flowers of the Chinese rose (Hibiscus rosa-sinensis) represent more than a beautiful plant. The Chinese rose has close links with religion and traditional customs. When these "flowers of beautiful dreams" are picked in the morning, they will not have wilted by the end of the day. Therefore it is not surprising that they are often worn in the hair, or used in buttonholes and sprays. The dye from the Chinese rose is used to make food and drink look more attractive, and in addition, some medicines are made with Hibiscus. In East Asia, the flowers are an essential part of the offerings taken along when visiting the temple.

BALI

Bali (Indonesia) is known as the island of ten thousand temples. There are signs of religion everywhere in the landscape of green mountains and rice paddies. The highest mountains, the volcanoes, the springs and oldest trees, are believed to be inhabited by spirits. It is precisely because the Balinese have built their temple complexes and holy places in the most magnificent spots that they have managed to safeguard the natural beauty of the island, and have even given it an extra dimension. ▶

TROPICAL RAINFOREST

The tropical rainforests and monsoon forests are essential for human life in many ways. They would be inexhaustible if the many products which come from the forests were used in a way that took the future into account. It is not only many consumer crops, but also a large proportion of the plants which adorn tropical gardens or are cultivated as greenhouse plants or pot plants in temperate zones, that originate from the jungle. Tree ferns, various palms, members of the arum lily family, bromelia plants, many ficus varieties and orchids - to mention just a few examples - all originate from the jungle.

ALSOPHILA SPECIES

Alsophila is a "tree fern." This collective name refers to various tree-shaped ferns from a number of families, including Dicksonia, Alsophila and Cyathea. The last two belong to the same family, and closely resemble each other. Like "ordinary" ferns, they are spore plants. The majority of tree ferns grow in areas with a constant high humidity. They are found at great heights in mountain forests, where the trees are shrouded in misty clouds. Some tree ferns, such as Alsophila australis, from Australia and Tasmania, can grow to a height of sixty feet in their country of origin.

A LSOPHILA SPECIES

HELICONIA ROSTRATA

Heliconias are adapted to be pollinated by butterflies and humming-birds, which are specialized in extracting the ample amounts of nectar from the flowers. The creatures are attracted by the bright-red color of the bracts. Many of the approximately one hundred and fifty species, which all originate from America, have become important as ornamental plants. This also includes Heliconia rostrata from Peru. The plant has long, hanging inflorescences one to two feet long, with two rows of bright-red bracts ending in a yellow point. In Africa and Central America, Heliconia rostrata is also cultivated for the art of flower arrangement. ▶

IPOMOEA HORSFALLIAE

Ipomoea horsfalliae is characterized by profuse blossoms which can last for months, as is characteristic of many diurnal varieties (Ipomoea species). The woody, climbing plant originates from tropical America, and is cultivated throughout the world, either as a garden shrub, or in greenhouses in temperate zones.

BROWNEA CAPITELLA

The flowerheads of Brownea capitella, a tree which originates in Venezuela, have a diameter of about ten inches. They hang from the ends of the branches like enormous colorful brushes.

CORDYLINE TERMINALIS "BELLA"

Because the leaves of this plant have beautiful colors, Cordylines are used on a large scale to produce colorful effects. Cordyline terminalis can grow to a height of ten feet, and its leaves can be up to two and a half feet long. The different cultivated varieties which have different colored leaves, include the red, variegated Cordyline terminalis "Bella."

VANDA TRICOLOR VAR. SUAVIS
The Indonesian islands of Java and Bali were the original habitats of Vanda tricolor var. suavis, an orchid with waxy flowers which exude a wonderful fragrance. It forms a stiff stem about three feet tall, covered with closely packed leaves, on which the inflorescences appear. Every flowering stem has five to ten white flowers marked with pink to deep purple blotches.

HIBISCUS ROSA-SINENSIS HYBRID
In the course of the centuries a large number of varieties of the Chinese rose have been cultivated (Hibiscus rosa-sinensis). There are varieties with double flowers which have a larger number of petals than the original species; the size of the flowers can differ, and there is an almost infinite variety of color. In addition to the well-known scarlet flower of the "common" Chinese rose, there are cultivated varieties with white, yellow, lilac, purple and red flowers in every hue.

COUROUPITA GUIANENSIS

When the large red flowers of the "Cannonball tree" or "forest calabash," as this tree is known in Surinam, are fertilized, it is many months before the round fruit is fully grown. They are the size of a man's head and can weigh thirteen to eighteen pounds. They have a rock-hard shell which is used by the native population in its original habitat as a gourd. When they fall to the ground and the hard fruit wall rots away, an evil-smelling fruit pulp is released containing large seeds. The Cannonball tree is indigenous to the South American rainforests. From there it was taken to other tropical areas long ago, and became extremely popular as an ornamental tree and as a curiosity. As can be seen in many trees at the bottom layer of the tropical rainforest, the flowers, and therefore eventually the fruit, appear on the trunk. This is known as cauliflorous growth.

SALACCA EDULIS

Salacca edulis which is indigenous to the Malaysian archipelago has beautifully shiny fruit covered with a hard shell. As the sour-sweet pulp of the fruit is edible, this bushy feathered palm is cultivated in its original habitat, and far beyond. The hard shell of the pear-shaped fruit consists of a large number of overlapping scales.

PHOENIX CANARIENSIS

Clusters of fruit on the Canary Island date palm (Phoenix canariensis). With the passing of the years the Canary Island date palm develops a tall ornamental trunk with an opulent, gracefully arched crown of leaves. The "true" date palm (Phoenix dactylifera), which is widespread in the dry tropics, and is one of the oldest cultivated plants, had a less spectacular appearance, though it is more valuable than the Canary Island date palm. The sweet edible dates of that palm have always been essential for the survival of nomadic people. Often the fruit was the only food available during their long treks. The leaf fiber was also used in the past to make rope and canvas, while the trunks of the date palm served as building material.

PLUMERIA RUBRA

Helicona Mariae

IPOMOEA ACUMINATA
There are an estimated four hundred Ipomoea species in tropical and subtropical zones. The popular name of the Ipomoea is "morning glory," because the flowers open at the crack of dawn and close up again in the afternoon. Ipomoea batatus, the sweet potato, is one of the most important sources of food in the tropics. Many of the species are cultivated as ornamental plants because of their climbing properties, their beautiful flowers and long flowering period. Ipomoea acuminata, from tropical America, can climb high up into trees and against tall fences with its winding stems. Its blue calyxes, which fade to lilac after a while, can be more than four inches wide.

CASSIA FISTULA
The Indian Shower of Gold (Cassia fistula) spread throughout the tropics from India and Ceylon to be cultivated as an ornamental tree. When it blossoms, the small tree has graceful hanging sprays of yellow flowers. After this, the long, dark brown, almost cylindrical pods develop. They can reach a length of one and a half feet and look rather like licorice sticks. They contain a sweet pulp in which the seeds are imbedded. In some regions this sweet "old man's licorice" is chewed. The seeds of the Indian Shower of Gold have a mild laxative effect and are sold as a purgative in western European countries. (Two other species: Cassia senna and Cassia angustifolia were important cash crops for centuries. They produced the medicinal and laxative senna pods and leaves.)

Brugmansia Suaveolens

Brugmansia varieties originate from South America, where they are found mainly in the Andes. In English they have the poetic name, "Angels' trumpet." Several Indian tribes, including the Mapuche in Chile, traditionally cultivated the shrubs and small trees for medicinal purposes. The seeds and other parts of the plant were also used to induce hallucinations. The Datura was cultivated for the same reason. Both these plants are members of the nightshade family. Although the Datura is not a shrub, but a herb-like plant, Datura and Brugmansia have so many characteristics in common that they used to be classified in the same genus. Brugmansia suaveolens (synonym: Datura suaveolens), which grows to a height of six to twelve feet, comes from the Amazon basin in Brazil, but it has been cultivated in many tropical regions where it has become commonplace. The enormous, bell-shaped flowers can grow to a length of seven to twelve inches.

TACCA CHANTRIERI

"Devil's flower," "Bat flower," "Cat's whiskers" are all popular names which arose in the attempt to describe the strange flowers of Tacca chantrieri in words. It is indigenous to Southeast Asia, where it is cultivated for its spectacular appearance. The plant forms a crown of large, beautifully marked leaves, with long stems, of which the sheaths overlap. The long stems of the flowers appear amongst the leaf stalks at the base. The purplish-brown flowers at the tops of the stems are surrounded by large bracts, while thread-like inner bracts up to a foot long form the "whiskers."

HELICONIA ILLUSTRIS "RUBRICAULIS"

Heliconias are not only popular for their beautiful flowers, but also particularly for their decorative leaves. When they have enough space, they form large, tall clumps of leaves which look attractive all year round. In the photograph shown here, Heliconia illustris "Rubricaulis" is planted on its own in a garden on the Indonesian island of Java. The long leaves of this cultivated variety are light green and a bright pinky or purplish-red color.

MUSSAENDA PHILIPPICA "ROSEA"

MUSSAENDA ERYTHROPHYLLA Mussaenda varieties are mainly woody plants with vertical or winding stems. They have small yellow, red or sometimes white star-shaped flowers which would not attract much attention if one of the sepals were not greatly enlarged and strikingly colored. The sepals can be bright red, pink, salmon-colored or white, and to a large extent determine the ornamental quality of the plant. One of the most beautiful varieties is Mussaenda erythrophylla, which grows to a height of thirty feet and comes from tropical West Africa. It has small flowers, with broad, scarlet sepals about three inches long. Mussaenda philippica has golden yellow flowers with five large, colored sepals. In the cultivated variety these are a pinky-red color, but there are also varieties with white sepals.

ERYTHRINA INDICA "PICTA"

Erythrina indica (synonym: Erythrina variegata) blossoms profusely and is indigenous on the Philippine and Indonesian islands where it is planted along roads and riverbanks, in parks and gardens, and to provide shade on coffee plantations. In Indonesia the leaves are steamed and are served as one of the dishes with the traditional "rijsttafel." The flowers contain a great deal of honey and are popular with birds which like the sweetness. As they fly from flower to flower, they pollinate them. The leaves of Erythrina indica "picta" have ornamental yellow veins.

RAVENALA MADAGASCARIENSIS

Where the leaf stalks of the Traveler's tree (Ravenala madagascariensis) enclose each other at the base, reservoirs of water are created which can hold more than a quart of moisture. This collects not only from rainfall, but is also secreted by the plant itself. When a hole is pierced in the leaf base, the moisture comes out and passers-by can drink it to quench their thirst, which is one reason for the name of the Traveler's tree. The notion that the fan of leaves indicates the points of the compass and can therefore serve as a signpost for travelers, is apparently very misleading.

PITCAIRNIA CORALLINA

Pitcairnia corallina from Colombia and Peru blossoms profusely in a shady spot where it has been planted as ground cover between the trees. The plant belongs to the bromelia family, of which the pineapple is by far the most familiar representative. As in other bromelias, the leaves of the approximately two hundred Pitcairnia varieties are arranged in rosettes. One of the varieties, Pitcairnia feliciana, is indigenous to Africa, and is therefore exceptional because virtually all the other bromelias originate from America. They are found there both in tropical rainforests and in dry regions.

X LAELIOCATTLEYA "EL CERRITO"

X Various related plant genuses are crossbred by specialist orchid growers with the intention of uniting the best qualities of several plants in a new species. The product of this sort of cross-fertilization is known as a sexual hybrid, and is identified with an "X" in front of its name. For certain orchids there is a natural tendency to hybridization, as in Laelia and Cattleya, which resulted in x Laeliocattleya.

DENDROBIUM "SRI SIAM"

Countless Dendrobium hybrids with the most diverse shapes and colors of flowers have been cultivated, particularly in Asia. They are not all suitable for garden plants. Many Dendrobium varieties are specially cultivated on a large scale as cut flowers. The flowers keep for a long time and are exported throughout the world.

INDEX